TOY ENGINEER

The Look Up Series #1

AMANDA

TOY ENGINEER

Real Women in S.T.E.A.M.

Aubre Andrus

"FOR THE GIRLS WHO ALWAYS DREAM ABOUT WHAT THEY'LL BE ONE DAY." — A A

Published by Adjective Animal Publishing in Santa Monica, California.

Visit us online at adjectiveanimalpublishing.com.

Design: Alice Connew
Photography: Ariel Moore
Logos: Shay Merritté
Illustrations: Aubre Andrus

12, Ducks: Joshua Coleman/Unsplash; Unicorns: June Gathercole/Unsplash; Toy truck: Michael Fousert/Unsplash; Robot: Phillip Glickman/Unsplash; Teddy: Sandy Millar/Unsplash; Wooden rings: Tomas Petz, Unsplash; 25, Paper clip illustration: Designed by rawpixel.com/Freepik; 26, Deming Hall: Cjeiler, Wikimedia Commons

Owleez is a trademark of Spin Master Ltd.

Library of Congress Cataloging-in-Publication Data is available upon request.

ISBN 9781639460007 (paperback)
ISBN 9781639460014 (hardcover)
ISBN 9781639460021 (e-book)

TABLE OF CONTENTS

Amanda

CHAPTER 1
MEET AMANDA

ℓ LET'S MAKE TOYS! ℓ

How do you make the impossible possible? Engineers answer this question every day.

I'm Amanda, and I'm an **engineer** at a toy company. I turn cool ideas into real toys that kids will love.

ENGINEERS SOLVE PROBLEMS WITH SCIENCE. Anything you can touch has been worked on by an engineer. That includes things like cars, video games, sneakers, and toys.

There are many different kinds of engineers. I'm a mechanical engineer. Mechanical engineers design, build, and test anything that moves. I work on toys that fly, drive fast, light up, or make noise like race cars, dolls, robots, fairies, helicopters, and more.

Working for a toy company is a lot of fun, but it's also a challenge. For example, how do you turn a motor and plastic into a puppy toy that walks and barks? These are the kinds of problems I tackle every day at work. But I love solving big problems.

I don't make toys on my own—I work with a team of engineers. It's easier to solve big problems with the help of others. I never have to solve a problem on my own. That's good because there are a lot of problems that we have to solve together along the way.

At toy companies, the engineering team works closely with other teams, like the toy design team. Toy designers show engineers sketches of **COOL** ideas. It's up to the engineers to decide if the idea is possible or not. At this point, the toy idea is usually a simple drawing on paper or the computer. But we have to imagine it as a real toy. We ask a lot of questions. Then we search for a lot of answers.

Is this idea awesome and unique?

Will it be easy to use? — This is always the first question we ask! If we're not doing something that will surprise and delight kids, we don't move forward with the idea.

Is this idea safe for all kids?

Could it be broken easily?

Will kids love it?

Could it be put together easily?

Sometimes, the answer to these questions is "no." It's easy for an engineer to say, "Sorry. That's a cool idea for a toy, but it's impossible."

But the most creative engineers don't say no. They think about what's possible. Then they think about how they can push what's possible further.

THAT'S HOW THE IMPOSSIBLE BECOMES POSSIBLE!

When someone says, "You can't do that," I say, **"YES, I CAN!"** That's the kind of thinking you need if you're going to be an engineer.

Can you think of a time that you solved a problem with the help of others?

ALL ABOUT AMANDA

I'm from... the suburbs of Chicago, IL
But now I live in... Los Angeles, CA

Summer or winter?
Summer

Dog or cat?
Both! I have cats but love all animals, even weird ones like opossum

Birthday: 16 July
Siblings: Two siblings, Katey and Dave
Pets: My cats, Mao and Chao

Ocean or mountains?
Mountains!

Cookies or ice cream?
Ice cream!

Favorite Color: Yellow
Favorite Food: Khao Soi (Thai Coconut Curry Noodle Soup)
Favorite Place: Yosemite National Park
Favorite City: Tokyo — they make very unique toys there that you can't find anywhere else!

What is your favorite thing about yourself?

I love adventures, trying new things, and sharing with the people I love. Whether it's experiencing new countries and cultures, trying new foods, or learning new hobbies, my curiosity is my greatest strength.

What makes you unique?

I speak my mind even when it's hard to do so or others might not agree. I believe that you have to challenge the status quo. Never do something just because "it's always been done that way."

Does anything scare you?

Sometimes, I'm scared people will think I'm not smart enough or creative enough to be an engineer or a team leader. Many people experience 'imposter syndrome,' where you are worried people will find out that you don't belong in your job. It's important to remember that you're so much stronger and more brilliant than even you might think. And you are deserving.

Who do you look up to?

My sister. She is strong and doesn't let small things bother her or distract her. She loves very generously, takes care of everyone in her community, and stands up for what she believes in.

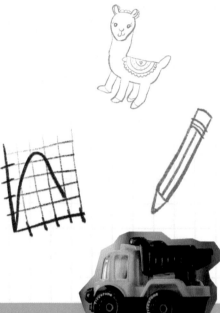

CHAPTER 2
HOW TOYS GET MADE

✒ BIG IDEAS ✑

One day, the toy design team showed the engineering team a big idea: **they wanted to make a toy owl that could fly**. My first thought was, *A toy that flies indoors? No way*. But then I started thinking harder.

Here are some questions that crossed my engineering mind:

How could we make this toy fly safely inside?

How can we make it affordable?

How will we make sure it doesn't break when it crashes?

How will all the mechanical parts fit inside?

How can we make this toy look like a real owl?

The engineering team sat down together. We started solving the problems one by one. Soon "no way" turned into "well, maybe…" Before we knew it, we were shouting, "Yes! We can do this!"

We had figured out how to make the impossible possible.

A toy owl sounds cool, but **what will it look like?** What exactly will it do? Once we know an idea is possible, we give the idea numbers and measurements.

A toy owl could fly for a short amount of time or a long amount of time. It could be heavy or lightweight. It could be small or large. Which traits should our toy have?

What is the shortest amount of time this owl can fly and still be fun?

It will fly for at least 30 seconds.

What is the most this owl could weigh but still be able to lift off the ground?

It will weigh at most 3 ounces.

How long should it take for the battery to charge? And how long will it last?

The battery will take at most 30 minutes to charge. It will last for at least one hour.

How small can this toy be while still fitting a motor inside?

It will be at least 7" tall.

Once we know how the toy should perform and look, then we can make a REAL-LIFE VERSION of the toy.

The sketches from the design team get turned into a prototype, which is an early sample of the toy. It's made by hand or printed on a 3D printer. It won't be perfect—**yet**.

Every product, from shoes to planes to theme park rides, starts with a prototype. The prototype may be a model, which is a smaller scale version, or it might be an exact copy.

The prototype will be slightly changed many times. It needs to perform the way we want it to. It needs to look the way we want it to. And we have to make sure that **kids love it**. This is where testing comes in—with real kids!

✐ THINK LIKE A KID ✐

I'm a grown-up, but I always try to think like a kid. I ask myself questions like, "Is this fun? Is this a toy I would have loved and wanted when I was a kid?" Toy engineers try to predict, or guess, what kids like. But it's much better to hear the truth directly from kids.

That's why we bring real kids and parents into our office. These kids get to see toys that no other kid has ever seen before. We don't ask, "Do you like this toy?" Instead, we **watch the kids play and listen to what they say.**

The testing room has a special mirror that's actually a window—and engineers sit secretly on the other side. We can see the kids, but they can't see us. We learn so much while we sit behind the two-way mirror.

Can you think of a time when getting feedback made you better at something?

We'll often change the toy a lot based on what the kids or parents said or did. My feelings aren't hurt if a kid says they don't like something. We want the toy to be the best it can be.

Sometimes, we base a new toy idea off something we learned

during testing. For example, we thought boys liked poop jokes more than girls did. But we learned that girls liked poop jokes just as much. So we created a **POOPING UNICORN** toy. It ended up being the number one toy for girls! We never could have guessed that without talking to real kids.

Here are some other interesting things we've learned about kids and parents:

Kids don't like toys that take forever to charge and then only work for a few minutes.

Parents don't like toys that take too long to put together and have lots of small parts.

Kids' tastes are always changing! Every year there is a new trend or a specific kind of toy that becomes really popular.

Parents don't like toys that are too messy or can only be used one time.

There are some toys that were popular with kids decades ago that are still popular with kids today. A really good toy idea is timeless.

Parents like toys that can teach their children something new.

AISLES FOR EVERYONE

Toy stores used to be divided into 'girl aisles' and 'boy aisles.' Now they are not. Kids can play with whatever toys they want to. There are no rules. Do you think toys should be labeled 'girl' or 'boy'? Why or why not?

✒ TO THE FACTORY ✒

Now that testing is done, our prototype is looking great. **There's just one catch:** we have to make 400,000 copies of this toy for kids around the world. But we can't make 400,000 toys by hand! Toys are made in a factory. Machines can piece together each toy much faster than any human could.

Another type of engineer, called a manufacturing engineer, works with a factory to create a sample toy. It's called a production sample. We make sure the production sample can do everything that the prototype can. Then we ask the factory to make **thousands** of more toys.

Every toy that is made in the factory will look exactly like the prototype we created by hand. It's kind of AMAZING! But these toys aren't ready for kids yet. **They have to pass a test first.**

When I visit a factory to see toys being made, I have to wear a hard hat, safety glasses, ear plugs, and steel toe boots.

The quality assurance team tests a sample toy from the factory. How? They play with it—**THE WRONG WAY**. This is called 'abuse testing.'

Quality engineers imagine **all of the things** a kid might do with this toy—even the things they aren't supposed to do. During safety testing, engineers might pull on the arm of an action figure to see if it breaks. Or drop a toy car from six feet high just to see what happens.

Why would we try to break our own toy? Because during every part of the toy-making process, engineers look for problems and create solutions—from the very beginning to the very end.

When we're done, we know that the toy is **AWESOME**, kids will have a great time playing with it, and it's safe for everyone.

TOY TESTING

Toys go through many different kinds of testing. During 'transit testing,' a machine shakes the toy for hours to make sure it doesn't break or fall out of the packaging. This means it will travel well in the back of a bumpy semi-truck to stores around the country.

FROM IDEA TO TOY STORE

1. The design team sketches an idea for a toy and presents it to the engineers.

2. The engineering team looks for problems and solutions. This is called a feasibility study. Feasibility means 'how easily can this be done?'

3. The model shop makes a prototype based on the design team's sketch.

4. The engineers list all of the materials that are needed to make this toy and how much it will cost. This is called a tool plan.

5. Real kids test the prototype and give feedback.

8. The factory sends one more toy, an 'engineering pilot,' to quality assurance for safety testing.

9. Engineers review the instructions to make sure they are easy to follow and understand. Kids need to know how to play with this toy and what to do with any accessories.

7. The factory makes just one toy, called a production sample. The engineers test the production sample against the 'master.' Then the factory can make hundreds of thousands—or millions—more.

10. The toys are shipped to stores around the world. Sometimes, they are first loaded onto boats and then trucks.

6. A manufacturing engineer decides how to make the prototype over and over again in a factory.

Here's the final flying owl toy!

Here I am with one of my favorite toys!

CHAPTER 3
HOW DID I GET HERE?

✐ SCHOOL DAYS ✐

When I was younger, I didn't even know what an engineer was! I was CREATIVE. Math and science weren't my strongest classes. But it turns out that my way of thinking was **perfect for engineering**.

As a kid, I loved building blanket forts, wrapping yarn around things, and watching my dad work on cars. My mom taught me how to crochet and sew. I liked using my hands to make things. We did a lot of baking at home, too. I loved turning one thing into another like when I turned flour, sugar, and water into a cupcake.

In school, I liked both science and art. In science class, I could mix chemicals to form a reaction. In art class, I could turn a blank paper into a burst of colors. At the time, I didn't realize how much I loved solving problems. But these kinds of challenges always excited me.

What do you love to do? What hobbies or activities make you happy?

That's exactly why I thought hard classes were more interesting. If I was really good at a subject, I found it boring. If I wasn't good at a subject, it kept my attention. I got frustrated when I couldn't figure out something in class. *Why can't I solve this?* But that feeling made me want to try even harder.

Physics homework and math homework took more of my time and energy. It wasn't easy. But it made the subjects more EXCITING. I knew I could always get better at math and science with some practice. When I finally solved a problem, **I felt proud**.

When a teacher tried to put me in a lower level science class, I disagreed. I could have gotten straight As in the easier class. But I wanted to be in the harder class where I could be challenged. I spoke up and then the teacher allowed me to join the more difficult class. That made me happy.

My love of problem solving was perfect practice for becoming an engineer. I didn't know this yet!

One day in high school, my computer teacher passed around a list of jobs and their salaries.

A salary is the amount of money you are paid each year to do a job. The jobs that made the most money were lawyers and doctors. But I didn't want to be a lawyer or a doctor.

The third career on the list caught my attention: **ENGINEER**. I had a vague idea what an engineer did. And I knew I could use both math and science as an engineer, which I liked. I also knew engineers made a lot of money. Because I grew up in a family with little money, this excited me. I made up my mind. *I'm going to be an engineer!*

This is me and my best friend Torrie at our high school graduation.

I ♡ SCIENCE

AMANDA'S UNIVERSITY

School: Rose-Hulman Institute of Technology
Location: Terre Haute, Indiana
Major: Mechanical Engineering

I ♡ ENGINEERING

～ OFF TO UNIVERSITY! ～

In elementary, middle, and high school, the teachers told us not to copy off other students. We weren't supposed to talk about our homework with classmates. In college, it was different.

My classes in college were COLLABORATIVE, which means we worked together to solve problems. This was good training for real life. In the real world, people work together to solve problems—especially when you're an engineer. Better solutions are found when creative people work together.

We worked in small groups on all of our homework assignments. When we turned in an assignment, we'd list all of our names on top so we could all get credit. It was awesome! **The students supported each other**, which means we helped one another get through tough times— and tough homework questions.

Have you ever worked on a group project? What was it like?

In college, you have to choose a major, which is a specific topic that you will study. There are many different kinds of engineering majors, and I had to choose one. I imagined what my job would be like for each major.

If I chose chemical engineering, I could move to France and create fragrances... If I chose electrical engineering, I could work in an energy processing plant... If I chose civil engineering, I could build a bridge in a big city...

I chose **mechanical engineering** because it was broad, which means it gave me a lot of options. Mechanical engineers are real-world problem solvers. Many companies are looking for problem solvers. I wasn't sure what kind of job I wanted, but I knew there would be a lot of jobs I could consider.

I also liked that mechanical engineering involved things that I could touch. An electrical engineer deals with electricity, which you can't often see or feel. But a mechanical engineer gets to work with machines and learns how to turn one thing, like a motor and plastic, into another, like a toy. It reminded me of when I used to bake and sew as a kid. I've always liked using my hands to make things.

TOP NOTCH

Rose-Hulman has been ranked the #1 Engineering college for more than 20 years, according to the U.S. News and World Report.

TYPES OF ENGINEERING

MECHANICAL ENGINEERS
design and create the mechanics that make objects move like drones, cars, planes, and rockets. This includes aerospace, automotive, wind, sound, and robotics engineering.

CIVIL ENGINEERS
design and build public structures like bridges, roads, trains, and water supply systems. This includes traffic, solar, and environmental engineering.

INDUSTRIAL ENGINEERS
combine engineering and business to keep industries safe, affordable, and organized. This includes safety, supply chain, manufacturing, and financial engineering.

ELECTRICAL ENGINEERS
design and create products that use or produce electricity like flashlights, computers, or satellites. This includes electronics, computer, and data engineering.

CHEMICAL ENGINEERS
design and create products made from chemicals like food and medicine. This includes paper, plastics, genetic, and food engineering.

WHAT IS COLLEGE?

Amanda has an undergraduate degree in mechanical engineering. Here's what that means and why she earned it.

Amanda went to college for four years after high school. In order to go to college, you must apply and get accepted. Good grades, volunteer experience, and letters of recommendation from teachers or community members can help you get accepted into a university.

People go to college to learn more about a specific career like mechanical engineering. After four years, if you've passed all of your classes, you get an undergraduate degree like Amanda did. It's a certificate that proves that you know a lot about a certain subject. Then you can put all that knowledge to use at a job.

WHAT IS A JOB?

Amanda's job is 'mechanical engineer.'
Why do people like Amanda have a job?

People work at a job in order to make money, which can be used to pay for a place to live, food, clothing, and fun things like travel and entertainment. Jobs give people a sense of purpose, or a reason to use their talents every day. Jobs can also make the world a better place by helping other people or by solving big problems. You can meet cool people and learn new things at a job.

Have you ever made money by doing a chore or task?

What are some careers that you can think of?

What kind of jobs do the people in your life have?

Going for
a long run
around Paris!

CHAPTER 4
AROUND THE WORLD

Canada

Sweden

Germany

France

Hong Kong

USA

Thailand

Taiwan

Mexico

Indonesia

ℓ TRAVEL FAR ℘

If you're interested in traveling or learning about cultures around the world like I am, engineering could be a great fit for you. **ENGINEERING HAPPENS ALL OVER THE WORLD!**

In my first toy industry job, I worked on toy race cars in Los Angeles, New York City, and Hong Kong. Then I moved back to Los Angeles and worked on dolls. After that, I moved to Toronto, Canada and got to work on all kinds of cool motorized toys.

As an engineer, you'll always work with people around the world. **Few products can be made in one place.** You might need to order some materials from one country then order some parts from another country. Then the product might be built somewhere else.

The toy industry is very global. We work with people in many different countries. Popular sand toys come from Sweden. In Mexico, many large playsets and outdoor playground equipment are built. Metal construction toys are made in France. And doll clothing is often sewn in Indonesia where BEAUTIFUL FABRICS are found.

I love working with people from other countries. You get to learn how people around the world work and think. It might be different from the ways you work and think. But that's great. Engineers try to solve problems that have never been solved before. The only way to do that is to gather a group of people that **THINK DIFFERENTLY THAN YOU**.

How we grow up affects how we think as adults. Kids are raised with different values. Values are the ideas that are most important to a person like kindness, honesty, or hard work. **Kids are also raised with different life experiences.** This includes where they live, where they went to school, and what their family is like.

When you are presented with a problem, you tend to solve it the same way over and over again. But when you work on a team with people who think differently from you, they can help push your thoughts in a new direction. You'll come up with ideas that you never could have come up with on your own. That's what I love most about engineering.

I'm PROUD of myself for taking risks and moving to new countries. All of my travels have helped me better

Our Hong Kong engineering team traveled to Indonesia for work

understand how kids around the globe play. Here are some interesting things I've discovered…

All around the world, handheld gaming is growing more popular for kids at younger ages. That means kids stop playing with toys and move onto video games earlier and earlier.

In Europe, kids play with certain toys a little bit longer than kids in the United States do. For example, a toy that is designed for a four year old in the United States might work for a six year old in Europe.

In China, parents want toys to teach a lesson. In the United States, we talk about how race cars are fast and fun. In China, we talk about how race cars teach the science of motion.

Action figures are very popular in Mexico.

Bathtubs aren't common around the world, so bath toys are usually only sold in North American countries like the United States and Canada.

TOY FAIRS

Toy engineers attend toy fairs to meet new people and learn about what's new and cool in the toy industry. Imagine an enormous building filled with rows and rows of toys from around the world—but you can't buy them! Each toy company sets up a booth that shows off their latest toy prototypes and technology. The biggest toy fair in the world is in Nuremberg, Germany.

✐ ON THE RUN ✐

I LOVE ADVENTURE—trying something new, exploring new places, and challenging myself. But I never imagined that I'd become a marathon runner when I grew up. It all started with **a very small goal**.

When I lived in Hong Kong, my apartment had a gym on the top floor. It had a beautiful view of a harbor. I liked to walk on the treadmill after work, so I decided to train for a 5K race. It's a run that's three miles (5 km) long. I didn't know if I'd ever be able to run for thirty minutes straight. I practiced three times per week. First, I walked. Then I ran short distances. **I GOT BETTER AND BETTER.** Six weeks later, I could run three miles!

On the day of the race, I noticed there were two courses: a shorter one and a longer one. I had trained to run the shorter 5K race. But others were running the longer 10K race. I thought, *That's impossible. How could they run twice as far as me? Well, maybe I could do that…*

After I finished the 5K race, I signed up for a 10K race—that's six miles (10 km). After I finished the 10K race, I felt

very proud of myself. But I could never have imagined running longer than that. Then a friend asked if I wanted to run a half marathon at a theme park in California. *Twice as long as my last race,* I thought. *Could I really run thirteen miles (21 km)?* **I HAD TO TRY.**

Soon my six mile runs turned into ten mile (16 km) runs. Running became a hobby of mine. Even while traveling for work, I had to squeeze in a practice run. Sometimes, the runs were more than an hour long. But I had made up my mind. I would—and could!—run a half marathon.

Every time I set out for a run, the distance felt like an impossible task. But when something feels impossible, it's much easier to chip away at it—one mile at a time. On the morning of the race, I felt excited and nervous as I ran alongside my friend and hundreds of others. Two hours later, I crossed the finish line. **I HAD DONE SOMETHING THAT I THOUGHT WAS IMPOSSIBLE.** It felt amazing.

As I held the medal in my hands, I couldn't help but think, *I've run a half marathon. Could I run a full marathon? Could I run twice as long as I did today?* I already knew the answer.

Over the next four months, I trained for the Los Angeles Marathon. That's twenty six miles (42 km). My daily runs went from twelve miles (19 km) to eighteen miles (29 km). I woke up the day of the marathon feeling STRONG. I was ready. At the start line at Dodger Stadium, I looked at the faces of all of the other runners. We were all about to turn something that felt impossible into something that was possible.

A year and a half before this, I didn't think I could run three miles. But four hours later, **I crossed the finish line of the marathon.** I had run from downtown Los Angeles all the way to the ocean in Santa Monica. I could run twenty six miles! It just took practice and hard work.

I signed up for another marathon in Chicago. And then three more in Toronto!

I feel like I can do anything now. Whenever I see a problem that seems impossible to fix, I know there's a very real chance that I can make it possible. And that makes me a better engineer.

Don't tell yourself that things are impossible. Start to chip away at it. Look at it from a different perspective. Or, talk to someone else about it and ask for help.

YOU'RE STRONGER THAN YOU THINK.

This is a map of my run around Paris!

AMANDA'S ADVICE FOR YOUNG ENGINEERS

FOCUS ON YOURSELF.

Don't let others define you. What's most important is that you are happy, healthy, and working toward your goals.

BUILD CONFIDENCE.

Know that not everyone is going to like all the decisions you make. Not everyone is going to believe in you. Find friends who want to support you, are proud of you, and think you are smart.

SIT WITH THE IMPOSSIBLE.

Just because you don't know how to tackle something today doesn't mean you won't know how next week. Sometimes I go to sleep thinking about a problem. Then I wake up with an answer. This happens a lot! It's a very cool feature of our brains.

DON'T HIDE WHAT MAKES YOU SPECIAL.

That is what will make you successful. It may feel like you're different, but the things that make you different are important. It might not seem this way now, but this is very true when you're a grown-up!

YOU CAN ALWAYS IMPROVE.

When you're having a hard time understanding something, don't get discouraged—ask for help! It's OK if something doesn't come easily to you. You might need it explained to you in a different way. Keep working at it until it clicks. You'll get there.

Researching monster trucks for future toys!

CHAPTER 5
YOU CAN BE AN ENGINEER!

TOY SCIENCE

Play is about more than just having fun. Play helps kids of all ages develop their bodies, their brains, and their feelings. Scientists have studied the many different ways kids play in order to learn what kinds of toys are best for each age range. After all, a two year old plays very differently than a twelve year old!

Engineers consider all of this when they work on a toy idea. They wonder which specific age group will play with the toy, how they will play with it, and why. Here are some things that scientists have learned about play at different ages:

Play helps babies and toddlers (ages 0-3) learn how to use their hands and solve challenges. This gives them independence, which is the ability to do something on their own.

Play helps younger kids (ages 4-6) learn how to use their imagination. They also learn how to be fair and help a friend whose feelings are hurt.

For older kids (ages 9-12), play can help them master a skill, which can give them confidence. This includes kicking a soccer ball into a goal, completing a science experiment, or painting a canvas.

❧ WAYS TO PLAY ☙

Every toy an engineer creates fits into a certain category and age group. That way every kid can find a toy they love. Below are some common toys organized by play type.

NURTURING PLAY

EDUCATIONAL PLAY

ROLE PLAY

ARTS & CRAFTS

CONSTRUCTION PLAY

MUSICAL INSTRUMENTS

GAMES & PUZZLES

Look at the toys in your room. Which play types do they fall under?

Which kinds of toys are your favorite and why?

Which toys were your favorite a couple of years ago?

ℯ BUILDING BLOCKS ℯ

Every toy has a **Bill of Materials (BOM)**. It's a list of parts and materials that are needed to make the toy. It's like the ingredients for a recipe. Grab one of your FAVORITE toys. **NOW, PRETEND THAT YOU NEED TO BUILD IT FROM SCRATCH.** List all the materials that you'd need using the charts on the opposite page. The BOM does not include the tools that are needed such as a needle, scissors, or pattern.

REVERSE ENGINEERING

Sometimes engineers don't know how to build something or don't know exactly how something works. When that happens, they take the item apart and look inside. 'Reverse engineering' helps them learn how to build something—and make it better.

ECO-FRIENDLY TOYS

There's too much plastic on our planet. But this is the perfect challenge for engineers to tackle! They could make toys with less plastic by mixing plastic with a natural material like bamboo. Or, toy companies could recycle old toys to make new ones. What other ideas do you have?

Toy Name: Stuffed Bear

Number	Part Name	Quantity	Purpose
001	plastic black beads	2	eyes
002	soft brown fabric	1/2 yard	fur
003	black thread	1 spool	to stitch the nose, mouth
004	brown thread	1 spool	to stitch body, arms, legs, head and ears together
005	stuffing	1/4 pound	To fill the body, arms, legs and head

Toy Name:

Number	Part Name	Quantity	Purpose

ℓ MONEY MATTERS ℓ

Engineers imagine how a toy works. But they also have to think about **how much it will cost.** Every feature on a toy costs money. Features include things like extra-soft fur on a stuffed llama or a remote control for a drone. Every feature must ADD VALUE, which means that it must be useful and important.

If a feature doesn't add value, engineers can remove it. This will lower the cost. But sometimes, engineers will replace that feature with a different feature that adds more value. Hopefully, it won't increase the cost. This process is called **'value analysis.'**

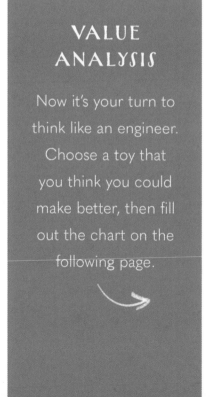

VALUE ANALYSIS

Now it's your turn to think like an engineer. Choose a toy that you think you could make better, then fill out the chart on the following page.

Toy Name: Marble Run

Features	30 blue plastic tubes, 3 yellow plastic ramps, 4 red plastic bases, 25 glass marbles, 10 plastic yellow spinners
Features that don't add value for me	I don't use the spinners. I have more marbles than I need. I don't like the colors.
Features that would add value for me	I would like more ramps. I would also like the tubes to be see-through instead of solid colored so I can see the marbles as they move.
Recommendation	Remove the spinners and reduce the number of marbles by 10. Instead, add 7 more ramps and make the tubes clear. I think this would cost about the same.

Toy Name:

Features	
Features that don't add value for me	
Features that would add value for me	
My recommendation	

✒ ENGINEER YOUR ✒ OWN IDEA

Now that you've learned about the types of play, what materials are needed to build a toy, and the value and cost of features, it's time to **DREAM UP YOUR OWN TOY IDEA.** There are a lot of questions to answer. You may find some problems along the way. **But no problem is too big to solve.** Remember, the IMPOSSIBLE IS POSSIBLE for engineers!

Need help getting started? Here's some inspiration…

Think about how you could make one of your favorite toys even better.

Design a toy your best friend would love.

Create a toy that will solve a problem or help you do something.

Dream up a cool accessory for one of your favorite toys.

Imagine what would happen if you mixed two toys together.

Draw a sketch of your toy idea.

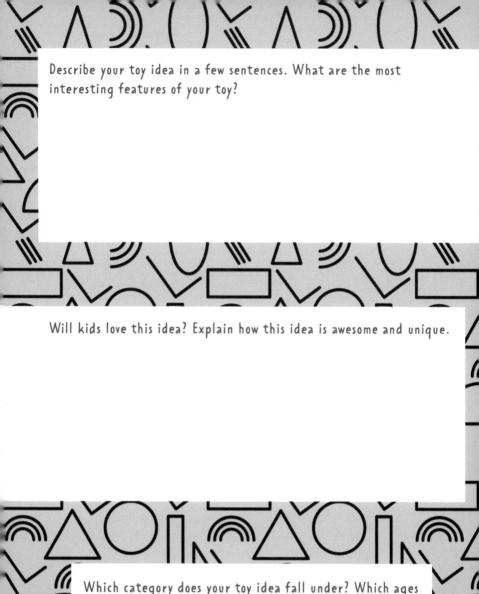

Describe your toy idea in a few sentences. What are the most interesting features of your toy?

Will kids love this idea? Explain how this idea is awesome and unique.

Which category does your toy idea fall under? Which ages will love this toy most? Hint: Look at 'Ways to Play' on page 44.

What materials are needed to build your toy? List all of them here.

Can it be put together easily? Describe any directions the toy will need.

Now write your own questions that are specific to your toy idea. Think like an engineer! Are there any risks or challenges that you will face?

My coworkers surprised
me with a birthday cake!

CHAPTER 6
LOOK UP!

I ♡ MATH

~ WHY WE LOOK ~
UP TO AMANDA

SHE'S SMART.

Even when she feels
stumped, Amanda
keeps trying.

SHE'S BRAVE.

Amanda has moved
all around the world
and isn't afraid to
try new things.

SHE'S STRONG.

Running a marathon
isn't easy, but Amanda
trained until she was
strong enough to cross
the finish line.

SHE'S CREATIVE.

Engineers use
science and math,
but they also have
big imaginations.
You can be great
at both science
and art.

SHE'S DETERMINED.

Amanda stays
focused on her goals
and doesn't let
anyone else hold her
back from reaching
her dreams.

Talk about a time you felt smart.

When have you felt brave?

Give an example of how creative you are.

What goals are you determined to achieve?

In what ways are you strong?

List all the things that make you special and unique.

LOOK UP MORE!

If any of the topics in this book inspired you, head to the library to find more information or ask an adult to help you search online. Here are some ideas to get you started.

ENGINEERING

Your local science museum may have some cool engineering exhibits and activities for kids. Young Engineers (**youngengineers.org**) and Engineering for Kids (**engineeringforkids.com**) hold workshops around the world and online.

RUNNING

Girls on the Run (**girlsontherun.org**) organizes more than 12,000 running groups across the United States for third graders up to eighth grade. Each group trains for a 5K, and runs a race together. Running a 5K race is exactly how Amanda got started.

TOY DESIGN

The Strong National Museum of Play (**museumofplay.org**) in Rochester, New York is dedicated to toys. You can visit the National Toy Hall of Fame and learn about historical toys that are hundreds of years old.

ABOUT THE EXPERT

Amanda Bright is the Sr. Director of Product Development Engineering at Spin Master, a global children's toy and entertainment company. In her role, she provides strategic leadership to a talented team of engineers who create both the toys of tomorrow as well as the processes by which the business evolves. Amanda is a mechanical engineer by training, having graduated from Rose-Hulman Institute of Technology. Both professionally and personally, she's motivated by challenging the status quo, holding leadership accountable, and advocating for the underrepresented.

ABOUT THE AUTHOR

Aubre Andrus is an award-winning children's book author with dozens of books published by American Girl, National Geographic Kids, Lonely Planet Kids, Disney, Scholastic, and more. Her titles encourage kids to be kind and be curious, and she is committed to writing books that empower girls and inspire them to become the leaders of tomorrow. Aubre received her degree in journalism and film from the University of Wisconsin. She currently lives in Los Angeles with her husband and daughter. Visit her website at **aubreandrus.com**.

WHO'S NEXT?

Meet Zi, a video game developer who was an artist before she was an engineer. Zi uses technology to transform ideas into games that entertain people around the world.

Visit The Look Up Series at www.thelookupseries.com to see who you can meet next and to find video interviews, free downloads for parents and educators, and more.

Made in the USA
Middletown, DE
15 September 2021